Gideon O'Grady was sitting on the banks of the river at Gravesend, watching passengers getting off the great ships.

"Good morning," said a cultured voice behind him.

Gideon leapt to his feet. A small, elegantly dressed lady wearing a red velvet gown was standing behind him. "May I sit with you for a while?" she asked politely. "I am rather tired."

"You're most welcome, ma'am,"

Gideon mumbled politely, wondering if he should bow or merely stand.

The lady coughed and sat down, fanning her face with a silk handkerchief.

"Please, retake your seat," she said, clearing her throat. The pearls in her tall hat glittered in the sun, like drops of rain on a spider's web.

"Thank you, ma'am." Gideon sat down stiffly.

"This is a charming spot," said the lady. "Do you often pass this way?"

Sam Godwin

MACDONALD YOUNG BOOKS

Gideon nodded. "Nearly every day. I come to watch the ships."

"I adore these great ships," the lady said. She loosened the stiff ruffle around her neck. "Have you ever been on one of them?"

Gideon shook his head. "I would like to be a captain on a galleon when I grow up," he said sadly, "but my friend Horatio says you can't be an officer unless you're from a titled family. I'll probably end up greasing the decks or bailing out the dirty water."

"I wouldn't take any notice of what people say," the lady said. She smiled, making her dark eyes sparkle like the pearls in her hat. "You can make any dream come true if you work hard enough. All you need is a bit of luck. I knew a little girl once who dreamt of crossing the sea. She had never been outside her country but she just KNEW there was a big exciting world out there, waiting to be explored. She achieved her dream too, even though it cost her a lot..."

Gideon stared at the lady. She seemed to have a faraway look in her eyes, as if she were casting her mind back across time and space.

"Who was she?" he whispered. "Will you tell me about her?"

Chapter 2

The lady coughed and cleared her throat. "The little girl was a princess, the daughter of King Powhatan who ruled over the tribes of East America. Most people called her Pocahontas but her real name was a secret. Only her family and close friends knew it."

"Why did she keep her name a secret?" Gideon asked.

"Your name is part of you," the lady explained. "If people knew it they could use it to harm you."

"I should like to have my own secret name," Gideon said. "Let me see, I would call myself…"

"You're a dreamer," laughed the lady, "just like Pocahontas. She used to spend a lot of time on the banks of the Powhatan River, pretending she was an eagle. She would let her spirit soar across the sea, towards new, exciting lands."

"That's what I do too," cried Gideon, "except that I pretend I am a captain on the prow of a ship."

The lady continued: "Pocahontas's friends thought she was mad. There is nothing across the sea, they insisted, no lands, no countries, no strange people with different clothes and customs. But Pocahontas just KNEW there was something beyond the vast ocean that circled the edges of her father's kingdom. She just felt it in her bones.

One evening, as Pocahontas was helping to sort out porcupine quills for embroidery, she was approached by an older lady of the tribe.

"The shaman wants to see you right away," the woman said.

Pocahontas shivered. The busy holy man only saw children when he had something important – or something horrible – to tell them. "What does he want?" she asked.

The woman shrugged. "I have no idea but he says it's terribly urgent. He's waiting for you in the longhouse."

Chapter 3

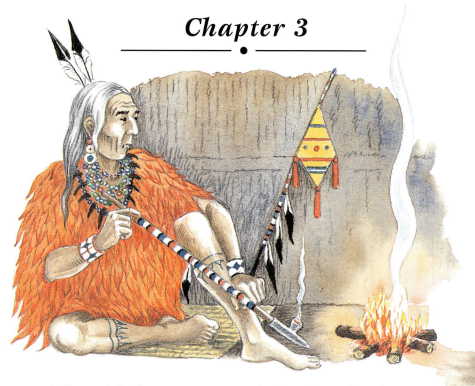

The old shaman was sitting by the fire,
smoking a clay pipe. "Sit down,
Pocahontas," he said.

Pocahontas sat down on a bearskin.

"Strangers have been seen on the
shores of our country," the shaman said.

Pocahontas looked up. "Strangers?
Where?"

"In Chesapeake Bay, they arrived on the backs of three strange birds. They have built some huts to shelter in."

Pocahontas could hardly contain her excitement. So she had been right after all. There were other lands across the sea. She smiled at the shaman. "Has anyone spoken to them yet?"

"They speak a strange tongue," the shaman informed her. "And they carry special weapons that kill with fire. I think they pose a great threat to our nation."

15

"They might be friendly," Pocahontas said.

The shaman shook his head sadly. "They have already invaded our sacred hunting grounds. They have killed some of our men too. Besides, there is the prophecy. It is said that a great wind will blow from the East to destroy our people. I fear these strangers are the first hint of that ill wind."

"It can't be," cried Pocahontas, standing up. "I won't let the strangers destroy us."

"What is meant to happen will happen," said the shaman. "We cannot change the future. But my dreams tell me that you will have an important part to play in this battle, Pocahontas. You shall bring peace between our nations." He threw a log on the fire. "Be brave, little princess, you are going to need all your courage to face the adventures that lie ahead of you."

The shaman closed his eyes and leaned back against the wall. Pocahontas realised that her audience with the holy man was over. Quietly she crept out into the night and walked slowly home. "I wonder what the strangers are like?" she thought. "I wonder what they eat and wear and what games their children play?" She paused to look back at the longhouse. "I wonder what country they come from?"

Chapter 4

Pocahontas sat with the other women of
the tribe in the big longhouse. The air
was thick with the smell of tobacco and
smoked fish. Rush mats had been spread
on the floor.

"The great chiefs are coming for a
meeting of the Powhatan tribes," one of
the women said.

Pocahontas watched as King Powhatan led the men into the longhouse. They had all painted their heads and shoulders with red dye. Bird feathers dangled from their long, dark hair. Their skin glistened with precious bear oil. It was obvious that they had come to a very important meeting.

"We must kill the strangers before they kill us," a chief said angrily. "They have built a fort on my tribe's hunting grounds."

"We must not be so hasty," argued King Powhatan. "They might only be here to trade and fish."

"They mean to stay here," snapped a brave. "They've been here for many moons, clearing the land and ploughing it."

"Nonsense," chipped in a younger brave. "Some of them have sailed away already. Only a few are left."

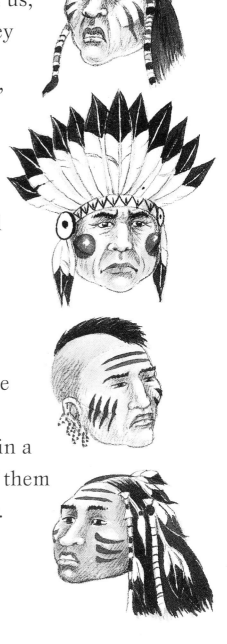

"Yes," said the first brave, "but the few that remain are exploring the land around them. I tell you they are looking for new places to settle in. One of their chiefs was caught upriver. What was he doing there?"

"Let's ask him," said King Powhatan. He called out and the prisoner was dragged in. He was short and a great beard obscured half his face. His skin was pale, as if he had lived his entire life in the dark. His green eyes scanned the longhouse, trying to make out the people in the gloom. Pocahontas's heart went out to him right away. How frightened, and yet how brave, he looked.

Powhatan nodded and women came forward with roast venison on a platter. The prisoner ate ravenously.

"Why are your people here?" asked Powhatan. "Do they mean to make this their land?"

"No," said the stranger, keeping his eyes firmly on the ground. "We are only looking for a way to the Pacific Ocean."

"He's lying," shouted a brave.
"Kill him," screamed another.

Suddenly two angry
braves grabbed the frightened
prisoner and pushed his head
to the ground. King Powhatan
raised a club studded with
sharp bear's teeth.

"No, father," Pocahontas cried. Before she could stop herself, the princess leapt to her feet and rushed towards the frightened stranger.

"Stand back," growled a brave.

"No." Pocahontas laid her head on the prisoner's. "I claim this man as my own."

Powhatan lowered the club. "She has a right," he said, "all Powhatan women can claim a prisoner as their own if they promise to look after him."

Pocahontas smiled shyly at the stranger. "Don't be scared of me," she whispered. "My name is Pocahontas. What is yours?"

Chapter 5

"John Smith," said Pocahontas to her friends. "His name is Captain John Smith and he comes from a powerful country across the sea, filled with stone houses. It is called England."

"England," repeated her friends, stirring the maple syrup in earthenware pots. "What a small name for a powerful country."

Many moons had passed since Pocahontas had saved the stranger's life. Since then she had been to his fort many times. She'd taken his starving men food and medicine. She'd helped sort out quarrels between them and the Powhatans. She'd even warned the inhabitants of the fort when her father had plotted to kill them. King Powhatan had threatened to disown her over that one.

"Will you go to England with John Smith one day?" asked a friend. Pocahontas nodded. "I'm sure I will."

29

Just then, a servant came running out
of the bushes. "Captain Smith is dying,"
she said. "He had a terrible accident."

Pocahontas put down her jar.
"When did it happen?"

"There was a fire on his boat," said
the servant, "he was injured and
cannot walk."

Pocahontas sent for herbs and the
bark of trees. Then she set out to the fort
right away, travelling by the light of the
full moon.

"You are too late," said the guard at the gate. "John Smith is dead. His body is on its way back to England for burial already."

Tears came to Pocahontas's eyes and a terrible wail escaped her lips. The basket of herbs slipped out of her grasp. John Smith was dead. Her best friend, her teller of tales was gone. She had no hope of seeing a different country now. Her dream would remain just that – a dream.

Chapter 6

Pocahontas was so upset over John's death that she ran away from home. With the princess gone, the English and the Powhatans started quarrelling bitterly again. King Powhatan ordered his men not to trade with the strangers. The English, desperate for food and crops, attacked villages and ransacked fields.

For nearly five years, Pocahontas lived in hiding on the banks of the Potomak River. She saw no one except a few friends.

Then, one day, a great ship came sailing past her hiding place.

"It's an English ship," her friend Jawatan said.

Pocahontas thought of John Smith and all he had told her about his country. "Are you sure?"

Jawatan nodded. "The captain has invited us on board for a meal."

"How wonderful," said Pocahontas. She accompanied Jawatan and his wife on board the *Treasurer*.

"I have heard a lot about you," said the captain, a burly man called Mr Argall. "You have become quite famous in England, Pocahontas." He served his guests a fine meal. Then he invited Pocahontas into the gun room. Suddenly the door slammed shut and the key turned in the lock.

"I am sorry I have to do this to you,
your highness," the captain said, "but
your father has stolen tools and weapons
from us. He has prisoners too. So we are
keeping you hostage until he returns our
men and property."

Chapter 7

Pocahontas was taken to Captain Smith's fort which was now called Jamestown. From there she was moved to a new English town called Henrico. A ransom note was sent to King Powhatan, but he did not reply.

At first Pocahontas was desperate. She missed the forest and the song of the birds. She hated washing in a bath instead of the river. "Is this where all my dreams have led to?" she wondered, "a little room in a crowded little town?"

But she was also fascinated by the strangers' way of life. Soon she started to wear their clothes, to learn their language and to attend church. She taught the English a lot about her culture too: she showed the women how to weave baskets, and how to cook baked beans and clams. Most important of all, she told the farmers when to sow crops and when to reap harvests.

One evening, while having dinner with the town's leader, she met a young tobacco grower called John Rolfe. He reminded her of Captain Smith but he was gentler and quieter.

"I hear you are becoming a Christian," said John Rolfe.

"Can I help teach you to read the Bible?"

"Yes," said Pocahontas, "I would like to know more about your country too. And I shall teach you about my people and their ways. You have a lot to learn from them."

Very soon the pair fell in love.

"Your father has just sent word that he is going to pay your ransom," John said to Pocahontas one evening as they walked along the banks of the river. "I can't bear the thought of losing you." He went down on one knee. "Will you be my wife?"

"I'd be honoured," Pocahontas said, "but what about your people? Will they accept me?"

"They will learn," said John, "it's your father I'm worried about. He might not take too kindly to his favourite daughter marrying an Englishman."

"Let's send him word," said Pocahontas. "Perhaps he'll say yes."

Messengers were dispatched to King Powhatan's court at once. For nine nail-biting days there was no reply. But on the tenth day, Pocahontas's own uncle came to Henrico with good news.

"King Powhatan has given his consent to the marriage," he said. "Let this union be a symbol of peace between our two nations. There shall be no more fighting between the Powhatans and the English."

Pocahontas smiled. The shaman's prophecy had come true. She had brought peace between the Powhatans and the strangers.

Chapter 8

Gideon looked at the lady. "And did Pocahontas ever come to England? Did she make her own dream come true?"

The lady laughed. "Yes. She was rewarded well for her good work. The wedding ceremony was held in a small church. Afterwards, John Rolfe took his bride to see the ships in the harbour. 'One day, I'll take you to see England,' he promised. And he did.

Pocahontas crossed the sea in a
mighty ship and sailed right past
Gravesend to London. People invited her
to dazzling parties. She starred in her
own play. She even met the queen."

Two women appeared
suddenly behind the lady,
their fans waving frantically.

"Madam," they chirped,
"we've been looking for you.
Are you all right?" They
scowled at Gideon.

"You're her, aren't you?" Gideon said.
"You're Pocahontas."

"I am indeed," laughed his companion.
"Now I must go. It is time for my
medicine." She lowered her voice. "I am
not well, they say."

Gideon smiled. "Thank you for telling me your story."

"I've enjoyed telling it," said Pocahontas, "I hope you will not give up your dream of becoming a sea captain now."

"I will not," Gideon promised. "With a bit of luck I too shall cross the sea."

Pocahontas stood up to leave. "We are friends now, so there is something else I want to tell you."

Gideon glanced at the frowning ladies. "What's that?"

Pocahontas leaned forward and whispered in his ear. "My secret name is... Matoaka."